ISBN 978-0-331-41853-8
PIBN 11121122

ANNUAL REPORTS

OF THE

TOWN OFFICERS

OF THE

TOWN OF EPSOM

FOR THE YEAR ENDING JANUARY 31, 1925

CONCORD, N. H.
EVANS PRINTING COMPANY
1925

TOWN OFFICERS

MODERATOR

WALTER H. TRIPP

SELECTMEN

GEO. E. HUCKINS, Term Expires 1925
ALBERT J. YEATON, Term Expires 1926
WALTER B. WELLS, Term Expires 1927

TOWN CLERK

MAURICE C. PHILBRICK

TREASURER

OLIVER C. LOMBARD

REPRESENTATIVE TO GENERAL COURT

FRED W. YEATON

COLLECTOR OF TAXES

EDWARD B. DEMERS

HIGHWAY AGENTS

District No. 1, JOHN W. COX
District No. 2, GEO. S. YEATON

SUPERVISORS OF THE CHECK LIST

MINOT R. YEATON   EDWIN R. YEATON
HARRY SILVER

OFFICERS OF THE SCHOOL DISTRICT

MODERATOR

LEWIS H. NUTTER

CLERK

HELEN YEATON

SUPERINTENDENT OF SCHOOLS

HENRY S. ROBERTS

SCHOOL BOARD

GRACE E. MARDEN, Term Expires 1925
HELEN T. RAND, Term Expires 1926
ELEANORA C. NUTTER, Term Expires 1927

TREASURER

ANNIE M. FOWLER

AUDITOR

OLIVER C. LOMBARD

TRUANT OFFICER

FRED W. YEATON

THE STATE OF NEW HAMPSHIRE

To the Inhabitants of the Town of Epsom, in the County of Merrimack, in said State, qualified to vote in Town Affairs:

You are hereby notified to meet at Town Hall, in said Epsom, on Tuesday, the 10th day of March next, at nine of the clock in the forenoon, to act upon the following subjects:

1. To choose all necessary Town Officers for the year ensuing.

2. To raise such sums of money as may be necessary to defray town charges for the ensuing year, and make appropriation for same.

3. To see if the Town will vote to give the Gossville Cemetery association the interest on cemetery trust funds intended for Gossville Cemetery.

4. To see if the Town will vote to observe the Two Hundredth Anniversary of the Town in 1927, and take any action relating thereto.

5. To see if the town will vote to discontinue the Tarleton Road so-called leading from the Mountain Road to a point in Babb Pasture, so-called.

6. To see if the Town will vote to authorize the Selectmen to have the main roads ploughed through the Town of Epsom during the winter with some approved power plow, the width and depth ploughed to be sufficient to accommodate the traffic.

7. To see if the Town will vote to accept the provisions of Chapter 117, Laws of 1917, on a section of the Suncook. Valley Road, so-called, and appropriate, or set aside from the amount raised for highway work the sum of $600.00 for this purpose.

8. To see if the Town will raise and appropriate the sum of $800.00 for State Aid Maintenance, the State to give $1,200.00.

9. To see if the Town will raise and appropriate the sum of $1,000.00 for Trunk Line Maintenance, the State to give $3,000.00.

10. To see if the Town will vote to raise and appropriate the sum of $2,500.00 and authorize the Selectmen to hire $3,000.00 if necessary to construct Trunk Line Bridge to replace the Iron Bridge over Suncook River at Gossville, the State to give $16,500.00 towards. construction of said bridge.

11. To see if the Town will vote to raise and appropriate the sum of $2,500.00 for construction of a section of the Suncook Valley or Central Road, the State to give $7,500.00.

12. To see if the Town will raise and appropriate a sum of money for the observance of Old Home Day.

13. To see if the Town will raise and appropriate a sum of money for the observance of Memorial Day.

14. To see if the Town will vote to raise and appropriate the sum of $160.00 as requested by the Library Trustees.

15. To see if the Town will raise and appropriate the sum of $400.00 for White Pine Blister Rust control.

16. To see if the Town will allow a discount on taxes paid on or before July 1st.

17. To transact any other business that may legally come before said meeting.

Given under our hands and seal this twenty-first day of February, in the year of our Lord nineteen hundred and twenty-five.

GEORGE E. HUCKINS,
ALBERT J. YEATON,
WALTER B. WELLS,
                    Selectmen of Epsom.

A true copy of Warrant—Attest:

GEORGE E. HUCKINS, .
ALBERT J. YEATON,
WALTER B. WELLS, ·
                    Selectmen of Epsom.

BUDGET OF THE TOWN OF EPSOM, N. H.

Estimates of Revenue and Expenditures for the Ensuing
Year January 31, 1925, to January 31, 1926, compared with Actual Revenue and Expenditures of the
Previous Year January 31, 1924, to January 31, 1925.

SOURCES OF REVENUE

	Actual Revenue Previous Year, 1924.	Estimated Revenue Ensuing Year, 1925.
From state:		
Insurance tax	$35.81	$35.81
Railroad tax	472.13	472.13
Savings bank tax	1,930.65	1,930.65
For highways:		
(a) For state aid maintenance		1,200.00
(b) For trunk line maintenance	851.24	3,000.00
Interest and dividend tax	21.88	21.88
Unimproved trunk line maintenance	575.77	600.00
From local sources except taxes:		
All licenses and permits except dog licenses	1,376.33	1,400.00
Rent of town hall and other buildings	5.00	
Rent of Webster Park	2.00	
Refund on insurance	35.70	
Rebate on tarvia, Barrett Co.	25.57	
Lewis Spurling Estate	37.92	
From poll taxes	1,886.00	
From other taxes except property taxes:		
(a) National bank stock	3.19	
Town clerk, candidates' fees	5.00	
Revenue applicable only to new construction and improvements:		

	Actual Revenue Previous Year, 1924.	Estimated Revenue Ensuing Year, 1925.
From state:		
State aid bridge	$827.56	
(b) For trunk line highway construction	8,697.72	
Amount raised by issue of bonds or notes	5,500.00	$5,000.00
Revenue which must be paid to other governmental divisions	163.60	160.00
Total revenues from all sources except property taxes	$22,453.07	
Balance in treasury	1,675.20	
Amount raised by property taxes	21,510.08	
Total revenues	$45,638.35	

PURPOSES OF EXPENDITURES

	Actual Expenditures Previous Year, 1924.	Estimated Expenditures Ensuing Year, 1925.
Current maintenance expenses:		
General government:		
Town officers' salaries	$905.00	$900.00
Town officers' expenses	173.68	200.00
Election and registration expenses	58.90	60.00
Care and supplies for town hall	288.21	200.00
Protection of persons and property:		
Dog damage	6.00	
Police department	133.83	100.00
Fire department	275.90	250.00

	Actual Expenditures Previous Year, 1924.	Estimated Expenditures Ensuing Year, 1925.
Health:		
Health department	$60.45	$50.00
Vital statistics	13.15	14.00
Highway and bridges:		
Unimproved:		
Town	575.77	600.00
State	557.67	600.00
State aid maintenance:		
State's contribution	925.99	800.00
Town's contribution		
Trunk line maintenance:		
State's contribution	859.24	3,000.00
Town's contribution	809.01	1,000.00
General expense of Highway department	6,201.24	5,000.00
Education:		
Libraries	310.00	160.00
Charities:		
Town poor	229.10	200.00
Patriotic purposes:		
Memorial day and other celebrations	50.00	50.00
Unclassified	449.50	400.00
Public service enterprises:		
Cemeteries	48.00	50.00
Interest:		
On temporary loans	162.91	150.00
Outlay for new construction and permanent improvements:		
Highways and bridges:		
Town construction	132.36	125.00

	Actual Expenditures Previous Year. 1924.	Estimated Expenditures Ensuing Year. 1925.
State aid construction:		
State's contribution Town's contribution.	$1,422.36	
Trunk line construction:		
State's contribution	8,697.72*	$16,500.00
Town's contribution	3,560.83	5,500.00
Discounts, abatements and **tax** sale	365.55	
Notes temporary	5,500.00	5,000.00
Payments to other governmental divisions:		
State taxes	1,909.00	1,909.00
County taxes	1,527.89	1,527.89
Payments to school districts	6,910.44	8,000.00
Soldiers' bonus	746.00	
Balance in treasury	1,780.65	
Total expenditures	$45,638.35	

* Bridge.

SELECTMEN'S REPORT

INVENTORY FOR 1924

No.

	Land and buildings	$595,765.00
187	Horses	19,640.00
16	Oxen	1,245.00
381	Cows	19,540.00
61	Neat stock	1,930.00
79	Sheep	459.00
1	Hog	14.00
29,549	Fowl	38,403.79
2	Portable mills	1,800.00
	Wood and lumber	21,991.00
4	Gasoline pumps and tanks	500.00
	Stock in trade	25,167.42
	Mills and machinery	32,500.00
376	Poll taxes at $5.00	$1,880.00
2	Poll taxes at $3.00	6.00
	Soldiers' exemptions	$2,340.00
	Amount of taxes	$23,615.57

APPROPRIATIONS, 1924

Highways and bridges, town maintenance	$4,401.27
Unimproved trunk line maintenance	650.00
State aid maintenance	600.00
Trunk line maintenance	900.00

Federal aid construction	$2,500.00
Town officers' salaries	900.00
Town officers' expenses	400.00
Town poor	200.00
Health department	100.00
Libraries	310.00
Cemeteries	50.00
Water hydrant service	200.00
All school purposes	8,072.00
Memorial Day	50.00
State tax	1,909.00
County tax	1,527.89
	$22,770.16
Overlay	845.41
Total	$23,615.57

Tax rate $28.50 on $1,000.00.

Respectfully submitted,

GEO. E. HUCKINS,
ALBERT J. YEATON,
WALTER B. WELLS,
                    Selectmen of Epsom.

ASSETS

Balance in treasury February 1, 1925	$1,780.65
Due from State	1,294.30
Due from Frank Sawyer, lumber	25.00
Balance on 1924 tax	216.48
Total	$3,316.43

LIABILITIES

Due School District, balance appro- priation	$2,322.00	
Due School District, 1924 dog tax	163.60	
Due on Knight case	35.80	
Total		2,521.40
Net assets to credit of Town		$795.03

LIST OF TOWN PROPERTY

Town hall—land and buildings	$2,000.00
Furniture and equipment	200.00
Library furniture and books	4,000.00
Tramp house	125.00

HIGHWAY DEPARTMENT

Land and buildings	750.00
Tools, machinery and supplies	1,000.00
Webster Park	1,000.00
Hearse	200.00
Watering troughs	150.00

SCHOOLS

Lands and buildings and equipment	6,000.00

TOWN CLERK'S REPORT

For Fiscal Year Ending January 31, 1925

Automobile registration permits	$1,376.33
Dog licenses	163.60
Candidates' fees	5.00
Total	$1,544.93

Paid Oliver C. Lombard, treasurer:

Auto registration permits, 1924	$800.29
Auto registration permits, 1925	576.04
Dog licenses, 1924	163.60
Candidates' fees, 1924	5.00
Total	$1,544.93

Respectfully submitted,

M. C. PHILBRICK, Town Clerk.

TREASURER'S REPORT

Balance in treasury, January 31, 1924 $1,675.20

M. C. Philbrick, 1924 auto permits	800.29
M. C. Philbrick, 1925 auto permits	576.04
M. C. Philbrick, dog licenses	163.60
M. C. Philbrick, candidates' fees	5.00
The Suncook Bank, by notes	5,500.00
State treasurer, insurance tax	35.81
State treasurer, railroad tax	472.13
State treasurer, savings bank tax	1,930.65
State treasurer, tax on interest and dividends	21.88
State treasurer, highway account	10,952.29
Rent of Town Hall and ball field	7.00
Estate of L. B. Spurlin	37.92
The Barrett Co., refund on tarvia	25.57
W. H. Tripp, refund on insurance premium	35.70
E. B. Demers, tax collector	23,399.27

Total receipts,	$45,638.35
Paid orders 201 to 375 inclusive	43,857.70

Balance in treasury, January 31, 1925 $1,780.65

Respectfully submitted,

O. C. LOMBARD, Treasurer.

SUMMARY OF RECEIPTS

RECEIPTS

Balance in treasury February 1, 1924	$1,675.20
Lewis Spurlin estate	37.92
M. C. Philbrick, Town Clerk, candidates' fees	5.00
M. C. Philbrick, dog licenses	163.60
M. C. Philbrick, automobile permits, 1924	800.29
M. C. Philbrick, automobile permits, 1925	576.04
State Highway Department:	
Federal aid construction	8,697.72
Trunk Line maintenance	851.24
Unimproved Trunk Line maintenance	575.77
State aid bridge (shoe factory)	827.56
Suncook Bank, temporary loans in anticipation of taxes	5,500.00
State treasurer, insurance tax	35.81
State treasurer, railroad tax	472.13
State treasurer, savings bank tax	1,930.65
State treasurer, interest on interest and dividends	21.88
Geo. E. Huckins, rent Webster Park	2.00
Geo. E. Huckins, rent Town Hall	5.00
W. H. Tripp, refund Library insurance	35.70
Edward B. Demers, collector, part 1924 taxes	23,399.27
Barrett Co., rebate on tarvia	25.57
Total receipts	$45,638.35

SUMMARY OF PAYMENTS

GENERAL GOVERNMENT

Detail 1, Salaries town officers	$905.00	
2, Expenses town officers	173.68	
3, Election and registration	58.90	
4, Town hall expenses	288.21	
		$1,425.79

PROTECTION OF PERSONS AND PROPERTY

5, Police department	133.83	
6, Fire department	275.90	
7, Damage by dogs	6.00	
		415.73

HEALTH AND SANITATION

8, Health department	60.45	
9, Vital statistics	13.15	
		73.60

HIGHWAYS AND BRIDGES

10, State aid maintenance	925.99	
11, Trunk Line maintenance	1,660.25	
12, Unimproved Trunk Line	1,133.44	
		3,719.68
13, Town road maintenance and general expenses Highway department	6,201.24	6,201.24

EDUCATION

14, Libraries	310.00	310.00

CHARITIES

15, Town poor $229.10 $229.10

PATRIOTIC SERVICES

16, Memorial Day 50.00 50.00

PUBLIC SERVICE ENTERPRISES

17, Cemeteries 48.00 48.00

ABATEMENTS REFUNDED

18, Abatements refunded 361.02 361.02

UNCLASSIFIED

19, Collins tax sale	4.53	
Blister rust, etc.	449.50	
Interest on temporary loans	162.91	
Trunk Line construction	12,258.55	
State aid, construction highways and bridges	1,422.36	
Town construction highways and bridges	132.36	
Temporary loans	5,500.00	
		19,930.21

PAYMENTS TO OTHER GOVERNMENTAL DIVISIONS

Detail 20, State treasurer, state tax	1,909.00
State treasurer, soldiers' bonus	746.00
County treasurer, county tax	1,527.89
School district, dog licenses, 1924	160.44

School district, part 1924
appropriation $6,750.00
                 ———————— $11,093.33

Total payments $43,857.70
Cash on hand at end of year   1,780.65

Grand total $45,638.35

DETAILED STATEMENT OF PAYMENTS

Detail 1—Salaries of Town Officers

Geo. E. Huckins, Selectman	$150.00
Albert J. Yeaton, selectman	125.00
Walter B. Wells, selectman	125.00
Oliver C. Lombard, treasurer	75.00
Maurice C. Philbrick, town clerk	50.00
Edward B. Demers, tax collector, part payment	200.00
Samuel R. Yeaton, auditor	5.00
Harry Silver, auditor	5.00
Minot R. Yeaton, supervisor	50.00
Edwin R. Yeaton, supervisor	50.00
Harry Silver, supervisor	20.00
Walter B. Wells, supervisor	30.00
Walter H. Tripp, moderator	20.00

                                    ———— $905.00

Detail 2—Expenses Town Officers

Edson C. Eastman, supplies	$11.53
Edward B. Demers, tax collector attending tax meeting	4.00
Albert J. Yeaton, general expenses	8.50
Geo. E. Huckins, general expenses	13.96

Geo. E. Huckins, telephone and postage	$3.98
Maurice C. Philbrick, miscellaneous	2.38
Geo. E. Huckins, miscellaneous	3.00
Albert J. Yeaton, miscellaneous	5.02
Walter B. Wells, general expense	8.40
Maurice C. Philbrick, printing, postage, etc.	12.78
Walter H. Tripp, bonding town officers	80.00
Albert J. Yeaton, assessors' meeting and selectmen's dinners	19.00
Geo. E. Huckins, postage and telephone	1.13

$173.68

Detail 3—Election and Registration

Evans Printing Co., check lists	$35.00
Geo. F. Mitchell, ballots and stationery	23.90

$58.90

Detail 4—Town Hall Expenses

Evans Printing Co., town reports	$241.71
Pembroke Water Works	7.50
Geo. E. Huckins, stamps, blanks, books and supplies	20.79
Albert J. Yeaton, miscellaneous	1.10
W. H. Knowles, supplies	17.11

$282.21

Detail 5—Police Department

Lewis H. Nutter, sheep killed by dogs	$6.00
Geo. E. Huckins, police work	17.93
Fred Meeks, police work	5.00
Geo. E. Huckins, police work	28.64
Albert J. Yeaton, care of tramps	10.10
Albert J. Yeaton, police work	19.30

Fred W. Yeaton, constable and ex-
penses $30.90
Walter B. Wells, police work 21.96

$133.83

Detail 6—Fire Department

Hydrant service $200.00
Nelson Emerson, watching fire,
Allie Bartlett's 3.00
Roy Taylor, watching fire, Allie
Bartlett's 3.00
Walter Sawyer, watching fire, Allie
Bartlett's 3.00
Harold S. Bickford, fire warden 7.00
C. O. Wells, deputy fire warden 15.80
J. C. Adams, Pittsfield fire department
attending fire at Allie Bartlett's 35.00
Silver and Young, chemical reloads 3.90
Geo. E. Huckins, use of auto and expense 5.20

$275.90

Detail 7—Health Department

Walter B. Wells, health officer $19.00
Walter B. Wells, health officer 23.45
L. D. Gilmore, M. D., Tallman case 4.50
Walter B. Wells, health work, postage,
expense, etc. 13.50

$60.45

Detail 8—Vital Statistics

L. D. Gilmore, reporting births and
deaths $5.00
Maurice C. Philbrick, reporting birth
and deaths 8.15

$13.15

HIGHWAYS AND BRIDGES

Detail 9—State Aid Maintenance

Charles E. Elliott, patrolman	$57.00	
Kidder Fisk, patrolman	278.43	
Aaron Osborne, patrolman	223.61	
Walter Wells	6.00	
Frank Gray	36.00	
Charles M. Steele	115.50	
Barrett Co., tarvia	209.45	
		$925.99

Detail 10—Trunk Line Maintenance

Geo. E. Huckins, freight on tarvia	$24.34	
Charles M. Steele	400.81	
Charles E. Elliott, patrolman	127.50	
Aaron Osborne, patrolman	497.79	
Kidder Fisk	529.81	
Frank Gray	80.00	
		$1,660.25

Detail 11—Unimproved Trunk Line Maintenance

Charles Elliott, patrolman	$638.64	
Kidder Fisk, patrolman	191.75	
Aaron Osborne, patrolman	303.05	
		$1,133.44

Detail 12—Town Road Maintenance

W. E. Yeaton, winter work	$233.91
B. M. Towle, winter work	491.57
Cyrus Marden, winter work	17.97
John W. Cox, road agent	2,191.75
Geo. S. Yeaton, road agent	1,750.00
Charles Elliott, washouts, etc.	268.81

Horace Bartlett, washouts, etc. $5.00
Bickford & Hnekins, lumber and supplies 382.52
Silver & Young, acct. John Cox, agt.   58.35
Silver & Young, supplies   2.02
Abel Lamprey, blacksmithing   20.03
Moses Q. Burnham, blacksmithing   81.65
Walter H. Tripp, insurance tool shed   2.50
W. H. Knowles, supplies   34.00
Aaron Osborne, work on roads   7.65
Kidder Fisk, work on roads   21.64
Berger Manufacturing Co., culverts   572.08
Charles N. Huckins, repairing road
  scraper and machine   3.25
Geo. E. Huckins, washouts, etc.   37.74
Albert J. Yeaton, washouts, etc   3.00
Page Belting Co., shaft for roller   5.80
Chas. H. Pike, repairing school sign   1.00
Chas. H. Palmer, watering trough, 1924   3.00
Frank Hurd, watering trough, 1924   3.00
Samuel R. Yeaton, watering trough, 1924   3.00
            ————— $6,201.24

Detail 13—Education

Library appropriations
For card index $100.00
For painting library   150.00
Maintenance   60.00
            ————— $310.00

Detail 14—Town Poor

O. C. Lombard, aid Sarah Abbott $183.85
Raymond Howard, hauling wood   3.50
C. O. Wells, wood furnished Sarah
  Abbott   29.75

John Moulton, hauling wood Sarah Abbott	$3.00	
Almon M. Worth, potatoes Sarah Abbott	7.50	
Walter B. Wells, potatoes Sarah Abbott·	1.50	
	———	$229.10

Detail 15—F. W. Yeaton, Memorial Day Committee

Appropriation	$50.00	$50.00

Detail 16—Cemeteries

Joseph Lawrence, mowing cemeteries	$20.00	
W. H. Knowles, attending funerals with hearse	28.00	
	———	$48.00

Detail 17—Unclassified

Edward B. Demers, tax collector, discount on taxes paid before July 1	$234.22	$234.22

Detail 18—Abatements

Fred Morris, property tax	$5.97	
Fred Morris, poll tax	5.00	
Maurice Zinn, poll tax	5.00	
Herbert Lovejoy, paid in Allenstown	5.00	
Mary Lovejoy, paid in Allenstown	5.00	
Five polls over 70 years	25.00	
Walter Pickard, horse tax	.72	
Lucy Bean, changed to Towle & Rand	21.38	
Heirs of Thomas Raymond, soldiers' exemption	6.17	
W. H. Towle & Bartlett, mistake in copying	43.28	
	———	$122.52

Detail 19

Edward B. Demers, tax sale of land and buildings, L. M. S. Collins	$4.53	$4.53

Detail 20

Peter Montminy, overtax	$4.28	$4.28

Detail 21—Blister Rust Control

J. H. Foster, state forester	$400.00	$400.00

Detail 22

Walter H. Tripp, bounty on hedgehog	$.25	$.25

Detail 23

M. C. Philbrick, auto permits	$49.25	$49.25

Detail 24

Suncook bank, interest on temporary loans	$162.91	$162.91

Detail 25—State Aid Construction Highways and Bridges

Chas. M. Steele, paymaster	$1,422.36	
John W. Cox, Demers bridge	132.36	
		$1,554.72

Detail 26—Federal Aid Construction

Charles M. Steele, paymaster	$12,030.45	
Chas. M. Steele, hauling and spreading sand	288.10	
		$12,258.55

Detail 27—Indebtedness

Paid Suncook bank, temporary loans	$5,500.00	$5,500.00

Detail 28

State treasurer, state tax	$1,909.00	$1,909.00
State treasurer, soldiers' bonus	746.00	746.00

Detail 28

County treasurer, county tax	$1,527.89	$1,527.89

Detail 29—School District, Annie M. Fowler, Treasurer

Balance 1923 appropriation	$1,000.00	
Part 1924 appropriation	5,750.00	
Dog licenses, 1923	160.44	
		$6,910.44
Grand total		$43,857.70

STATE OF NEW HAMPSHIRE HIGHWAY DEPARTMENT

STATE AID MAINTENANCE

	State	Town	Total
Appropriation, 1924	$900.00	$600.00	$1,500.00
Extra appropriation	833.88	278.00	1,111.88
Total fund	1,733.88	878.00	2,611.88
Expended	1,733.88	878.00	2,611.88

UNIMPROVED TRUNK LINE ROAD

	State	Town	Total
Appropriation, 1924	$650.00	$650.00	$1,300.00
Expended	586.27	586.27	1,172.54
Balance for 1925	63.73	63.73	127.46

TRUNK LINE MAINTENANCE ACCOUNT

	State	Town	Total
Appropriation, 1924	$2,400.00	$800.00	$3,200.00
Expended	2,340.50	780.17	3,120.67
Balance for 1925	59.50	19.83	79.33

REPORT OF B. M. TOWLE, ROAD AGENT

Paid Hollis Hall, team, 14 hours	$10.89
Hollis Hall, labor, 26 hours	8.58
Arthur Sullivan, labor, 6 hours	2.00
Hill, ½ hour	.50
Guy C. Pike, shovel, 10 2-3 hours	3.50
Clayton Mason, team, 15 hours	11.70
Horace Bartlett, team, 15 hours	11.70
John Yeaton, team, 27 hours	21.00
John Yeaton, labor, 7½ hours	2.50
C. S. Seaward, 22 hours	7.33
J. Laurence, team, 6 hours	4.67
J. Laurence, labor, 7 hours	2.33
L. H. Nutter, team, 8 hours	6.22
L. H. Nutter, labor, 25 hours	8.33
Charles Palmer, team, 6 hours	4.50
Charles Bickford, team, 23 hours	17.87
Herbert Ethridge, team, 4½ hours	3.00
Towle, team, 21 hours	16.33
Rand, team, 21 hours	16.33
Fred Durgin, team, 54 hours	42.08
Phillip Morrill, labor, 10 hours	3.25
Arthur Sherburne, labor, 13 hours	4.33
Albin Ambrose, team, 18 hours	14.00
Hollis Hall, team, 28 hours	21.97
Frank Brown, labor, 18 hours	6.00
Albert Ordway, labor, 6 hours	2.00
P. R. Eaton, team, 35½ hours	27.61
P. R. Eaton, labor, 43½ hours	14.50
Charles Bickford, team	4.66
Charlie Hazen, team, 13 hours	10.11
Roscoe Kelly, labor, 38 hours	12.67
E. M. Kelly, team, 45 hours	35.00

Paid E. M. Kelly, labor, 9 hours	$3.00
Geo. O. Locke, 1 horse and man, 27 hours	15.00
Geo. O. Locke, labor, 3 hours	1.00
Ernest Clarke, labor, 27 hours	9.00
S. L. Clarke, team, 27 hours	21.00
Leon Clarke, labor, 9 hours	3.00
Frank P. Wheeler, labor, 46 hours	15.31
Frank P. Wheeler, team, 72 2-10 hours	56.30
Ralph Carter, labor, 10 2-3 hours	3.50
E. Demers, labor, 10 2-3 hours	3.50
Frank Sawyer, labor, 10 2-3 hours	9.50
	$191.89

REPORT OF W. E. YEATON

WINTER WORK, 1924

Frank E. Brown, team	$3.50
Frank E. Brown, labor	6.00
S. R. Yeaton, team	14.00
S. B. Haynes, labor	.67
E. R. Yeaton, labor	.67
Raymond Howard, labor	5.33
N. H. Monroe, team	7.78
N. H. Monroe, labor	6.67
E. L. Heath, team	22.56
George Yeaton, team	6.23
George Yeaton, labor	1.33
Will Morgan, labor	5.00
E. R. Yeaton, horses	6.67

Frank E. Hurd, team	$22.56
Earl Marden, labor	3.00
J. T. Libby, labor	12.00
S. E. Hardy, labor	4.50
S. E. Hardy, team	10.50
Winthrop Fife, labor	4.84
Clifton Fife, labor	1.33
E. A. Philbrick, team	10.89
E. A. Philbrick, labor	2.00
A. B. Cass, team	10.89
A. B. Cass, labor	3.67
George Moulton, team	3.50
W. E. Yeaton, labor	10.00
Fred Yeaton, team	10.89
Fred Yeaton, labor	1.00
C. O. Wells, team	8.56
S. B. Haynes, labor	3.17
N. M. Cofran, labor	.67
Fred Butler, labor	1.85
Ward Boehner, labor	1.17
Howard Bickford, team	2.33
Warren Fowler, team	6.22
Warren Fowler, labor	2.67
George Haynes, labor	2.00
George Haynes, team	5.44
E. C. Straw, labor	1.85

$233.91

REPORT OF C. M. STEELE, FEDERAL AID PROJECT NO. 181

EXPENSE HAULING AND SPREADING SAND FOR TOWN

B. M. Towle, team	$17.89
B. M. Towle, foreman	15.00
George Huekins, team	14.00
Henry Ames, team	16.33
Arthur Sherburne, labor	7.50
Charles Davis, labor	9.00
Nelson Emerson, labor	8.00
A. L. Brown, labor	8.00
William McKenzie, labor	8.00
Claude Huckins, labor	7.00
Arthur Huckins, labor	6.00
Kenneth Hnekins, labor	5.00
Lewis Hill, labor	8.17·
Lewis Hill, labor	5.20
Fred W. Yeaton, labor	3.00
Arthur Demers, labor	2.00
Ernest Sullivan, labor	5.17
Moses Randall, labor	2.00
Maurice Yeaton, labor	2.00
Ernest Kelly, labor	2.00
Raymond Ring, labor	2.00
Roy Guptill, labor	2.00
Clyde Guptill, labor	2.00
Clifton Spurlin, labor and use of auto	7.17
Fred Ames	2.00
C. M. Steele, foreman	16.50
E. C. Annis, 104 loads of sand	10.40
Howard Tolman, labor	3.17
Ernest Taylor, labor	3.17
Frank Hatch, labor	3.00

Lauren Smith, labor $1.67
Aaron Osborne, labor   11.88
Kidder Fiske, labor   11.88
                                                   ─────────────
    Total payments $228.10

Received from town   · $228.10

C. M. STEELE,
Foreman.

───────────

REPORT OF C. M. STEELE, FEDERAL AID PROJECT, NO. 181

Henry Ames, team $256.84
George E. Huckins, team   257.50
Clayton Mason, team and labor   .   108.06
Frank E. Hurd, team and labor   195.22
Fred W. Yeaton, team and labor   94.89
Horace Bartlett, team and labor   87.67
B. M. Towle, foreman and team   399.50 ·
B. M. Towle, use of engine and auto   15.00
A. L. Brown, labor   136.67
Nelson Emerson, labor   120.00
Russell Yeaton, labor   31.50
Peter McKay, labor   48.00
Kenneth Huckins, labor   52.67
Arthur Huckins, labor   13.50
Claude Huckins, labor   3.00
Arthur Sherburne, labor   169.95
C. M. Steele, foreman   309.50
C. M. Steele, cash paid out   5.00
L. Pickard, labor   15.00

Walter Pickard, labor	$66.00
Frank Mahoney, labor	15.40
Michael McAdoo, labor	12.40
John Clarke, labor	135.34
Leon Clarke, labor	124.84
Ernest Clarke, labor	85.50
Charles Carson, labor	95.00
Charles Davis, labor	114.72
William Reynolds, labor	10.50
Leon Ordway, labor	12.00
Roscoe Warren, labor	81.00
Ernest Kelly, labor	30.00
W. A. Sawyer, labor	78.95
E. Zinn, labor	60.00
George Pike, labor	77.20
Carl Schulz, labor	25.00
Frank Hatch, labor	84.40
William McKenzie, labor	82.67
Clifton Spurlin, labor	60.00
Lewis Hill, labor	9.00
Bickford & Huckins, hauling sand	110.00
Bickford & Hnekins, lumber and supplies	153.90
H. P. Maxfield & Co., dynamite and supplies	127.71
Silver & Young, cement and supplies	154.26
C. N. Huckins, gasoline and grade pins	8.25
W. S. Langmaid, gravel	50.00
William Rogers, labor	135.70
Albert J. Yeaton, trucking and labor	20.86
Kate Etheridge, board McAdoo and Mahoney	25.20
Robert Carpenter, damage	5.00
James Steele, use of auto	2.00
Frank Ambrose, use of auto	1.50
Gerald Marden, labor	43.55
Louis Demers, labor	24.00
Arthur Demers, labor	24.00

Augustus Brown, labor $18.00
Edgar Annis, labor 85.00
Ernest Sullivan, labor 9.00
William Yeaton, labor 43.95
Charles Gordon, labor 12.00

Total payments $4,633.27

Received from town $4,621.83
Received for dynamite 11.44

Total $4,632.27

STATEMENT ON CONTRACT FEDERAL AID, NO. 181

Amount of contract $16,548.35
Extra work 166.03

Total amount $16,714.38

Amt. expended by town (1923) $10,480.58
Amt. expended by town (1924) 4,621.83

Total $15,102.41
Actual profit to town 1,611.97
$16,714.38

Total amount $16,714.38

REPORT OF C. M. STEELE, FEDERAL AID
PROJECT, NO. 201-B

Henry Ames, team	$370.49
George Huckins, team	447.62
George Huckins, gravel, auto and labor	11.65
B. M. Towle, foreman	385.00
B. M. Towle, gravel	50.30
B. M. Towle, use of engine and auto	19.00
Frank Hurd, team and labor	170.34
Horace Bartlett, team and labor	369.30
Howard Bickford, team	342.23
Fred Davis, team and labor	112.39
Karl Rand, team	170.34
Charles Palmer, team	109.28
Clayton Mason, team	124.84
Lucas Clarke, team and labor	70.01
C. M. Steele, foreman	413.00
C. M. Steele, cash paid, telephone and postage	12.25
Kenneth Huckins, labor	182.84
Claude Huckins, labor	51.34
Arthur Huckins, labor	56.67
Lewis Hill, labor	204.35
Leon Waterhouse, labor	191.86
Gerald Marden, labor	145.68
Frank Little, labor	12.00
George Pike, labor	146.01
Charles Davis, labor and care of lights	147.52
Frank Hatch, labor	163.84
W. J. Rogers, labor	81.34
Walter A. Sawyer, labor	31.84
Walter A. Sawyer, damage to land and build-ings	35.00
Elmer Palmer, labor	59.34
Philip Morrill, labor	150.17

Warren Hamilton, labor	$139.34
Fred Ames, labor	175.68
Howard Tolman, labor	49.50
Herbert Bickford, labor	6.00
C. N. Huckins, gas	5.57
James Steele, labor	2.00
Leroy Fernald, operator air compressor	37.00
A. L. Brown, labor	148.67
Leon Clarke, labor	145.67
Arthur Sherburne, labor	88.67
Earl Marden, labor	46.67
William James, labor	62.67
John Mcdonald, labor	151.17
Ernest Clarke, labor	157.17
Albert J. Yeaton, use of auto and labor	6.40
Frank Hall, gas and labor	11.60
John Clarke, labor	22.67
Silver & Young, cement and supplies	45.97
Maurice Clarke, labor	96.67
Charles Carson, labor	81.17
Raymond Carson, labor	78.00
Charles Erickson, labor	27.00
W. H. Knowles, tools and supplies	132.10
H. P. Maxfield & Co., dynamite and supplies	187.25
F. E. Everett, use of air compressor and blasting wires	66.00
Earl Griffin, labor	66.00
Nelson Emerson, labor	61.50
Frank Lakin, labor	64.00
Louis Demers, labor	23.50
Charles Gordon, labor	32.00
Harry Osborne, labor	15.00
L. D. Gilmore, medical attendance	1.00
Concord Foundry & Machine Co., C. B. grate	8.50
Sarah Bartlett, sand	21.00

Edgar Annis, sand		$3.00
C. K. Marden, damage to buildings		10.00
Bickford & Huckins, dynamite, fuse and lumber		352.68

Total payments		$7,466.63

Received from town	$7,408.62	
Received sale dynamite and fuse	53.01	
Use cement mixer	5.00	
		$7,466.63

STATEMENT ON CONTRACT, FEDERAL AID, NO. 201-B

Amount of contract		$9,030.00
Work estimated to Nov. 1, 1924	$6,471.50	
Work done since Nov. 1, 1924	1,200.00	
		7,671.50
Money expended		7,408.62
Tools, dynamite, etc., on hand		250.00

REPORT OF C. M. STEELE

STATE AID ACCOUNT

Lewis Hill, labor	$7.50
Lewis Hill, mileage	3.00
Louis A. Demers, labor	6.00
Arthur Demers, labor	3.00

Ernest Sullivan, labor	$7.50
Moses Randall, labor	3.00
Maurice Yeaton, labor	3.00
Kenneth Huckins, labor	3.00
Laurence Tasker, labor	3.00
William E. Yeaton, labor	6.00
Ernest Kelly, labor	3.00
Raymond Ring, labor	3.00
Ernest Taylor, labor	4.50
Howard Tolman, labor	4.50
Clifton Spurlin, use of auto	5.00
Clifton Spurlin, labor	7.50
C. M. Steele, foreman	16.00
Leland Gray, labor	3.00
John Stimmell, labor	3.00
John Stimmell, use of auto	2.00
Roy Guptill, labor	3.00
Clyde Guptill, labor	3.00
Willie Brown, labor	3.00
Fred Ames, labor	3.00
James Steele, labor	1.50
James Steele, use of auto	2.50
Arthur Sherburne, labor	3.00

$115.50

Received from town $115.50

C. M. STEELE, Foreman.

REPORT OF C. M. STEELE, TRUNK LINE
. MAINTENANCE ACCOUNT

Frank Hurd, team	$21.00
George Huckins, team	21.00
B. M. Towle, team	7.00
Henry Ames, team	21.00
F. W. Yeaton, team	21.00
Charles Palmer, team	21.00
Louis Demers, team	14.00
John Yeaton, team	14.00
J. B. Osborne, team	14.00
G. L. Clarke, team	14.00
C. M. Steele, foreman	26.00
Louis Demers, labor	3.00
Arthur Demers, labor	4.00
Augustus Brown, labor	6.00
Clifton Spurlin, labor	10.00
Ernest Sullivan, labor	16.00
William McKenzie, labor	13.00
Charles Carson, labor	9.00
Roy Taylor, labor	6.00
Leon Ordway, labor	6.00
James Steele, labor	6.00
Lewis Hill, labor	11.50
Lewis Hill, use of auto	4.00
Plummer Demmeritt, labor	6.00
Ernest Frederick, labor	4.67
Howard Tolman, labor	6.00
Carl Schulz, labor	3.00
Kenneth Osborne, labor	10.67
Kenneth Huckins, labor	8.67
Moses Randall, labor	1.00
Maurice Yeaton, labor	1.00

Ernest Kelly, labor	$1.00
Raymond Ring, labor	1.00
Roy Guptill, labor	1.00
Clyde Guptill, labor	1.00
Fred Ames, labor	1.00
Nelson Emerson, labor	1.00
A. L. Brown, labor	1.00
C. S. Hall, team	21.00
Ernest Taylor, labor	6.00
W. H. Knowles, shovels as per bill	15.00
Ellen A. Ayers, sand, 128 loads	12.80
J. E. Philbrick, sand, 95 loads	9.50
	$400.81
Received from town	$400.81

C. M. STEELE, Foreman.

REPORT OF C. M. STEELE ON STATE AID BRIDGE ACCOUNT

Preston M. Bailey, foreman	$210.00
H. S. Palmer, labor	112.00
John Clark, labor	56.00
Leon Clark, labor	56.00
Raymond Carson, labor	70.53
Charles Carson, labor	9.00
Claude Huckins, labor	3.67
Kenneth Huckins, labor	10.22
Raymond Ring, labor	9.00

Nelson Emerson, labor	$6.00
Ernest Sullivan, labor	3.50
John Bickford, labor	9.00
C. H. Davis, labor	1.67
W. A. Sawyer, labor	1.55
Lewis Hill, labor	1.55
Henry Ames, team	16.33
Geo. Huckins, team	3.89
B. M. Towle, team	21.00
C. M. Steele, paymaster	14.00
Bickford & Huckins, as per bill	347.74
Connelly Co.	69.50
C. N. Huckins, gasoline	2.95
B. & M. R. R., freight	61.74
A. J. Yeaton, trucking	1.00
Frank Hall, labor	1.00
Silver & Young, cement and supplies	282.71
Kittredge Bridge Co., supplies	24.30
Geo. E. Huckins, as per bill	15.25
American Express Co., as per bill	1.26

$1,422.36

Received from town $1,422.36

C. M. STEELE, Paymaster.

STATE OF NEW HAMPSHIRE HIGHWAY DEPARTMENT

TOWN OF EPSOM

S. A. Bridge, 1924 Account

Money available	State	Town	Total
Total fund	$1,000.00	$1,344.80	$2,344.80
Expended	1,000.00	1,344.80	2,344.80

EXPENDITURES

Date	Item	Paid by Town	Paid by State	State to Town
June 28.	Steele, C. M.	$124.88		
July 1.	James, eng.		$4.00	
July 5.	Steele	130.02		
July 12.	Steele	268.46		
July 29.	James, eng.		6.00	
May 31.	Harvey Co., reinforced steel		36.60	
July 30.	State highway truck, No. 19		25.00	
Aug. 4.	State highway, 12 channels, only		27.19	
Aug. 4.	1 channel, 26 wood fillers, 1 bolt cutter		11.63	
July 19.	Steele	433.18		
July 26.	Steele	465.82		
July 19.	Bailey, P. M.		20.00	
	I beams $682.63, freight $57.37, carting $10.00	750.00		
	Bailey		17.12	
	Langley, bridge eng.		4.99	

July 19. State truck, moving
        machinery $20.00
Jan., 1925.   Check to town $827.56

      Total footings $2,172.36 $172.44 $827.56

REPORT OF JOHN W. COX, ROAD AGENT
DISTRICT NO. 1

WINTER AND SPRING WORK

E. M. Kelley, team, 36 hours	$28.00
E. M. Kelley, labor, 41 hours	13.67
Roscoe Kelley, labor, 36 hours	12.00
Geo. Kelley, labor, 18 hours	.6.00
A. N. Ambrose, team, 30½ hours	23.72
A. N. Ambrose, labor, 28½ hours	9.50
Frank Wheeler, team, 35½ hours	27.61
Frank Wheeler, labor, 33½ hours	11.17
H. M. Carter, team, 32½ hours	25.28
H. M. Carter, labor, 58½ hours	19.50
Herbert Etheridge, labor, 27 hours	9.00
William Etheridge, labor, 27 hours	9.00
Arthur Sherburne, labor, 2 hours	.67
John J. Yeaton, team	3.00
Chester Seaward, labor	23.34
J. W. Cox, labor, 77 hours	42.77
Louis Demers, team, 21 hours	16.33
Louis Demers, labor, 34½ hours	11.50
Joseph Lawrence, team 8 hours	6.22
Joseph Lawrence, labor, 20½ hours	6.84
Hollis Hall, team, 30 hours	23.33

Hollis Hall, labor, 27 hours	$9.00
Fred Duguay, labor, 95 hours	31.67
Joe Duguay, labor, 87 hours	29.00
J. E. Philbrick, team, 4 hours	2.40
Frank E. Brown, labor, 18 hours	6.00
	$406.52

REPORT OF J. W. COX, ROAD AGENT
DISTRICT NO. 1

Paid George H. Huckins, team, 9 hours	$7.00
Arthur Huckins, labor, 9 hours	3.00
F. W. Yeaton, team, 9 hours	7.00
H. W. Etheridge, labor, 9 hours	3.00
C. H. Palmer, team, 96 hours	74.66
C. H. Palmer, labor, 27 hours	9.00
Warren Hamilton, labor, 31½ hours	10.50
Ernest Taylor, labor, 16 hours	5.33
C. S. Hall, team, 9 hours	7.00
Walter Sawyer, labor, 6 hours	2.00
S. L. Clark, team, 90 hours	70.00
S. L. Clark, labor, 13½ hours	4.50
John Clark, labor, 9 hours	3.00
Leon Clark, labor, 9 hours	3.00
Ernest Clark, labor, 81 hours	27.00
Harold Locke, labor, 18 hours	6.00
Fred Kimball, labor, 27 hours	9.00
Horace Bartlett, team, 31½ hours	24.50
Henry Ames, team, 9 hours	7.00
Clayton Mason, team, 36 hours	28.00
P. R. Eaton, team, 4½ hours	3.50
P. R. Eaton, labor, 4½ hours	1.50

Paid Neil Reid, labor, 9 hours $3.00
     Peter McKay, labor, 4½ hours   1.50
     E. J. Place, labor, 42 hours   14.00
     Frank Wheeler, team, 235½ hours   183.17
     Frank Wheeler, labor, 124½ hours   41.50
     Chas. Hazen, team, 16 hours   12.44
     E. M. Kelley, team, 12 hours   9.33
     E. M. Kelley, labor, 59 hours   19.67
     Geo. Kelley, labor, 54 hours   18.00
     Roscoe Kelley, labor, 214½ hours   71.50
     John P. Yeaton, team, 135 hours   105.00
     John P. Yeaton, labor, 58½ hours   19.50
     J. B. Osborne, labor, 135 hours   45.00
     Lewis Demers, team, 95 hours   73.89
     Lewis Demers, labor, 122¾ hours   40.81
     W. J. Rogers, labor, 102 hours   34.00
     Clarence Hart, labor, 99 hours   33.00
     Hollis Hall, labor, 82 hours   27.33
     John W. Cox, labor, 563 hours   312.76
     Arthur Sherburne, labor, 21 hours   7.00
     Leon Waterhouse, labor, 24 hours   8.00
     A. N. Ambrose, team, 122 hours   94.89
     A. N. Ambrose, labor, 85 hours   28.33
     Lewis H. Nutter, team, 111 hours   86.33
     Lewis H. Nutter, labor, 3½ hours   1.17
     Joseph Lawrence, team, 72 hours   56.00
     Joseph Lawrence, team only, 67½ hours   30.00
     Joseph Lawrence, one man, 57½ hours   19.17
     J. E. Philbrick, team   15.00
     Fred Duguay, labor, 69 hours   23.00
     B. M. Towle, use of engine   10.00
     Geo. E. Huckins, 80 loads of gravel   8.00
     H. W. Etheridge, 11 loads of gravel   1.10
     Lewis H. Nutter, 55 loads of gravel   5.50
     Louis Demers, 25 loads of gravel   2.50

Paid C. M. Steele, dynamite	$4.20
For tools and bolts	4.15
	$1,785.23

REPORT OF G. S. YEATON, ROAD AGENT
DISTRICT NO. 2

George Moulton, 201 hours, team	$156.33
Leon Ordway, 141 hours, labor	47.00
George Dutton, 318½ hours, labor	106.16
Samuel Yeaton, 14 hours, team	10.89
Samuel Yeaton, 40½ hours, labor	13.50
Fred Stone, 18 hours, team	14.00
Fred Stone, 18 hours, labor	6.00
Russell Yeaton, 67 hours, labor	29.78
Russell Yeaton, man 54 hours, labor	18.00
Edgar Wells, 387½ hours, labor	129.16
Raymond Howard, 108 hours, team	84.00
Eugene Philbrick, 29 hours, labor	9.66
Eugene Philbrick, 8 hours, team	6.22
John Jawoeska, 9 hours, labor	3.00
Herbert Bickford, 90 hours, labor	30.00
Winthrop Fife, 9 hours, labor	3.00
Norman Munroe, 27 hours, labor	9.00
Norman Munroe, 40 hours, team	31.00
Fred Yeaton, 18 hours, labor	6.00
Frank Hurd, 26 hours, team	20.22
Samuel Haynes, 13 hours, labor	4.33
Anson Cass, 15 hours, labor	5.00
Anson Cass, 3 hours, team	2.33
Grover Stevens, 13½ hours, labor	4.50
Charles Elliott, 18 hours, labor	9.50

B. H. Fowler, 61½ hours, labor	$20.50
B. H. Fowler, 103½ hours, team	80.49
Fred Lear, 32 hours, labor	10.67
Lewis Hill, 27 hours, labor	9.00
Kenneth Huckins, 27 hours, labor	9.00
James Libbey, 85½ hours, labor	28.50
Scott Hardy, 81 hours, team	63.00
J. E. Plante, 54 hours, labor	18.00
C. O. Wells, 36 hours, team	28.00
E. R. Yeaton, 99 hours, team·	77.00
G. S. Yeaton, 299½ hours, team	232.87
G. S. Yeaton, 325½ hours, labor	144.68
Maurice Yeaton, 124 hours, labor	41.33
·Maurice Yeaton, 10½ hours, team	8.00
Fred Yeaton, 27 hours, team	21.00
Albert Brown, 18 hours, labor	6.00
Howard Bickford, 3 hours, labor	1.00
Howard Bickford, 139 hours, team	108.11
Albert Stevens, 3 hours, labor	1.00
C. M. Steele, dynamite	11.00
Federal Aid, 181, dynamite	11.44
Albert Ordway, gravel, 100 loads	10.00
S. R. Yeaton, gravel, 16 loads	1.60
Fred Fife, gravel, 20 loads	2.00
Frank Smith, gravel, 65 loads	6.50
G. S. Yeaton, gravel, 280 loads	28.00
G. S. Yeaton, lumber	12.00
·Blacksmith, sharpening picks	.75

$1,750.00

Received from town $1,750.00

GEORGE S. YEATON,
Road Agent, District No. 2.

REPORT OF PINE BLISTER RUST ACCOUNT

FINANCIAL STATEMENT

1924 town appropriation	$400.00	
State aid	100.00	
Balance 1923 town and state funds	2.15	
Total available		$502.15
Crew wages	$481.46	
Expenses	18.50	
Total expended		$499.96
Balance town and state funds		2.19
Town balance	$1.75	
State balance	.44	
Area covered		2,176 acres
Average cost per acre		$0.229
Currant and gooseberry bushes destroyed		83,954
Pine infections located		188

REPORT OF THE TRUST FUNDS OF THE TOWN OF EPSOM, JANUARY 31, 1925.

For Perpetual Care of Cemetery Lots

Date of creation	Trust Funds—Purpose of Creation	How Invested	Amount of principal	Rate of Interest	Balance of income on hand at beginning of year	Income during year	Expended during year	Balance of income on hand at end of year
Mar. 2, 1903	John L. Brackett, by self	In Savings Bank	$50.00	4 %	$ .33	$2.00	$2.00	$ .33
" "	S. M. ——, by	"	50.00		1.32	2.04	2.00	1.36
" "	J. A. Clough,	"	50.00			2.00	2.00	
June 1, 1907	Mary A. Swain, "	"	50.00	4½ %	1.75	2.04	1.00	2.79
Mar 26, 1912	Susan E. P. Forbes, "	"	200.00	4 %	28.87	10.26	5.50	33.63
Feb. 15, 1915	William Murphy, "	"	25.00	3 %		1.00	1.00	
" 18, 1915	Abbie Hopkinson, "	Received in bond	1,000.00	4 %	14.48	30.00	2.00	42.48
" "	C. F. ——,	In Savings Bank	50.00		.45	2.00	2.00	.45
" "	(Gen.) B. L. Locke, by James L. L. ——	"	50.00		.70	2.00	2.00	.70
" "	Morrill Hoyt, by Ebenezer Hoyt	"	50.00		.45	2.00	2.00	.45
" 15, 1917	Mary B. L. Dowst, by self	"	100.00		7.97	4.28	4.00	8.25
" "	Horace Bickford, "	"	100.00	4½ %		4.50	4.00	.50
" "	Hiram Holmes, "	"	100.00		4.38	4.68	4.00	5.06
" "	Henry Knox, "	"	100.00	4 %	4.34	4.68	5.00	4.02
Mar. 28, 1917	Sara E. Burnham,	"	50.00		4.94	2.16	3.00	4.10
" 27, 1917	—— N. Holmes, (John Wallace lot and Wallace row), by self	"	100.00		3.91	4.63	4.63	3.91
Aug. 29, 1917	Mary A. Evans, by self	"	400.00	4½ %	34.17	19.53	14.75	38.95
Nov. 9, 1917	—— ——, by	"	50.00		.16	2.25	2.00	.41
Jan. 25, 1918	John T. Cotterell, by Clara A. Cotterell	"	100.00		7.89	4.81	1.25	11.45
" "	William Sanders, "	"	50.00		2.79	2.34	.75	4.38
June 25, 1920	Eliza J. Bickford, by self	"	100.00		2.05	4.59	4.75	1.89
Aug. 27, 1921	John M. ——,	"	100.00		6.99	4.77	1.00	10.76
" "	Sophila S. Bul—— ——,	"	50.00		2.75	2.34	2.00	3.09

Date	Name	Investment	Amount	Rate				
Sept. 26, 1922	Daniel T. Cilley, by Annie L. Towle	In Savings Bank	50.00	4½ %	....	2.25	2.00	.25
" "	John and Salome Babb, by Annie L. Towle	" "	50.00	"	....	2.25	2.00	.25
Jan. 21, 1924	Hilton Goodhue, by Mrs. C. H. Kempton	" "	75.00	"	....	3.09	3.00	.09

For Painting and General Up-keep of Iron Fence at South Side of McClary Cemetery

Date	Name	Investment	Amount	Rate				
Jan. 21, 1924	Mary A. Evans	In Savings Bank	229.66	4½ %	....	10.30	....	10.30

For Benefit of Epsom Public Library

Date	Name	Investment	Amount	Rate				
Apr. 5, 1908	Benjamin F. Webster	Received in bond	1,000.00	4 %	197.50	46.81	57.70	186.61
Sept. 21, 1914	(Dr.) Orrin S. Sanders	In Savings Bank	100.00	5 %	51.85	7.55	....	59.40
May 3, 1916	Susan E. P. Forbes	{ U. S. Government Bonds }{ In Savings Bank }	2,000.00	{ 4½% }{ 4½% }	194.53	91.44	94.05	191.92
July 30, 1917	Mary A. Evans	In Savings Bank	500.00	4½%	34.01	24.03	....	58.04

This is to certify that the information contained in this report is complete and correct, to the best of our knowledge and belief.

JOHN C. BROWN,
ELLERY C. STRAW,
JOSEPH LAWRENCE,

Trustees of Trust Funds.

We hereby certify that we have examined the accounts of the Trustees of the Trust Funds of the Town of Epsom, and find them correctly cast and supported by proper vouchers.

SAMUEL R. YEATON,
HARRY SILVER,

Auditors.

Epsom, N. H., February 7, 1925.

AUDITORS' REPORT

ASSETS

Balance in treasury, February 1, 1925	$1,780.65
Due from state on federal aid construction	1,294.30
Due from Frank Sawyer, lumber	25.00
Balance on Edward B. Demers' tax list.	216.48
Total	$3,316.43

LIABILITIES

DUE SCHOOL DISTRICT

Balance, 1924 appropriation	$2,322.00	
1924 dog tax	163.60	
Due on Knight case	35.80	
		2,521.40
Net assets to credit of town		$795.03

We hereby certify that we have examined the accounts of the Selectmen, Clerk, Treasurer, and Road Agents of the town of Epsom, and found them correctly cast and supported by proper vouchers.

SAMUEL R. YEATON,
HARRY SILVER,
Auditors.

REPORT OF MEMORIAL DAY COMMITTEE, 1924

Received from C. M. Steele, balance from 1923 $1.09

Received from town treasurer   50.00

    $51.09

Paid Rev. H. H. Appelman, speaker $15.00

Paid Colburn Girls' orchestra   15.00

Paid flags   20.00

    50.00

      Balance on hand $1.09

FRED W. YEATON,
Committee.

REPORT OF HEALTH OFFICER

Time and expense quarantining and reporting contagious diseases	$28.00
Abating nuisance	1.50
Investigating septic tank nuisance at Gossville school	1.50
Time and expense of two delegates to the Health Institute at Durham as required by law	15.00
Trip to Concord with water and milk samples (typhoid test)	6.45
Postage and telephone	3.50
Total	$55.95
Received of town	$55.95

Respectfully submitted,

WALTER B. WELLS,
Health Officer.

Epsom, N. H., January 31, 1925.

REPORT OF CEMETERY TRUSTEES

RECEIPTS

Balance at the beginning of the year	$84.14
Savings Bank interest	4.37
Trustees of Trust Funds	79.63
Town of Epsom	20.00
Sale of lots	35.00
Total receipts	$223.14

EXPENDITURES

Care of lots	$79.63
Mowing and raking McClary cemetery	20.00
Improvements	4.00
Balance in Savings Bank	119.51
Total	$223.14

PAID FOR CARE OF LOTS

Horace Bickford lot	$4.00
Hiram Holmes lot	4.00
Henry Knox lot	5.00
John T. Cotterell lot	1.25
William Sanders lot	.75
Walter Chesley lot	2.00
Susan E. P. Forbes lot	5.50
Mary B. L. Dowst lot	4.00
Sarah N. Holmes lot and Wallace Row	4.63

J. L. Brackett lot	$2.00
C. F. Griffin lot	2.00
S. M. Chesley lot	2.00
J. A. Clough lot	2.00
B. L. Locke lot	2.00
William McMurphy lot	1.00
Morrill Hoyt lot.	2.00
Mary A. Swain lot	1.00
Flora E. Burnham lot	3.00
Hopkinson and Marden lots	2.00
Mary A. Evans (2) lots	14.75
Eliza J. Bickford lot	4.75
John M. Moses lot	1.00
Sophila Bulfinch lot	2.00
Daniel T. Cilley lot	2.00
John and Salome Babb lot	2.00
Hilton Goodhue lot	3.00
	———
	$79.63

Respectfully submitted,

JOHN C. BROWN,
ELLERY C. STRAW,
JOSEPH LAWRENCE,
Cemetery Trustees

Epsom, N. H., January 31, 1925.

We hereby certify that we have examined the accounts of the Cemetery Trustees of the Town of Epsom and find them correctly cast and supported by proper vouchers.

SAMUEL R. YEATON,
HARRY SILVER,
Auditors.

Epsom, N. H., February 7, 1925.

REPORT OF SCHOOL BOARD

For the Fiscal Year Ending June 30, 1924

Received as per Treasurer's Report   · $11,148.98

EXPENDITURES

Salaries of district officers	$95.00
Superintendent's excess salary	133.00
Truant officer and school census	40.00
Expenses of administration	69.67
Teachers' salaries	4,040.00
Text books	85.61
Scholars' supplies	51.26
Flags and appurtenances	18.25
Other expenses of instruction	1.62
Janitor service	99.80
Fuel	255.00
Water and janitor's supplies	10.39
Minor repairs and expenses	393.26
Transportation of pupils	566.25
High School and Academy tuition	1,000.00
Elementary school tuition	252.00
Insurance	69.30
Construction of addition to Gossville schoolhouse	2,973.95
New equipment	511.15
Payment of interest on debt	40.00
Tax for state-wide supervision	230.00
Payment of bills from previous year	175.00

Total $11,110.51

Balance on hand June 30, 1924 $38.47

PAYMENTS IN DETAIL

A. H. Martel, construction at Gossville	$200.00
A. H. Martel, construction at Gossville	200.00
B. M. Towle, cash paid A. H. Martel	100.00
A. H. Martel, construction at Gossville	200.00
A. H. Martel, construction at Gossville	100.00
A. H. Martel, construction at Gossville	200.00
School District of Chichester, tuition for three pupils	108.00
Elbridge Bartlett, janitor service	17.00
A. H. Martel, construction at Gossville	200.00
A. H. Martel, construction at Gossville	200.00
A. H. Martel, labor and material	500.00
John B. Varick Co., flags	15.73
L. D. Gilmore, M. D., medical inspection	50.00
Loella M. Wells, salary as teacher	72.00
Katharine Coulson, salary as teacher	85.00
Katherine Chase, salary as teacher	85.00
Evelyn E. Clark, salary as teacher	60.00
Olga H. Peterson, salary as teacher	65.00
Doris M. Kenison, salary as teacher	60.00
Ada F. Little, cleaning New Orchard school-house	5.00
Albion N. Ambrose, cleaning vault at Center	.80
Lawrence Tallman, labor	.50
John B. Varick Co., two box stoves	52.20
Ryan and Buker, supplies	8.25
J. L. Hammett Co., Hyloplate blackboards	61.22
American Seating Co., 24 desks and chairs	223.20
John B. Varick Co., metal ceiling	28.80
Charles H. Pike, repairs, New Rye, Gossville and Short Falls	101.72
George P. Kelley, transportation	50.00
Gedeon Petit, installing closets at Gossville	151.56

A. H. Martel, labor and material	$500.00
Loella M. Wells, salary	72.00
Katharine Coulson, salary	85.00
Katherine Chase, salary	85.00
Evelyn E. Clark, salary	60.00
Olga H. Peterson, salary	65.00
Doris M. Kenison, salary	60.00
A. A. Mooney Furniture Co., six window shades	13.50
Bailey Lumber Co., moulding	3.30
Osgood & Co., stove pipe, etc.	9.47
Union School District of Concord, tuition, three pupils, one-half year	105.00
C. H. Pike, paint and labor at Gossville	119.92
H. S. Roberts, expense hiring teachers	29.30
H. S. Roberts, books	3.45
George P. Kelley, transportation	45.00
Edward E. Babb & Co., supplies	.75
John B. Varick Co., two flag-poles and holders	2.52
Harry Houston, writing lessons	2.57
J. L. Hammett Co., supplies	37.77
Silver Burdett & Co., text-books	11.20
Emma P. Clough, treasurer of supervisory union, superintendent's excess salary	133.00
George E. Farrand, state treasurer, per capita tax	230.00
Silver and Young, shingles and supplies	100.00
Loella M. Wells, salary	72.00
Katharine Coulson, salary	85.00
Katherine Chase, salary	85.00
Doris M. Kenison, salary	60.00
Evelyn E. Clark, salary	60.00
Olga H. Peterson, salary	65.00
Walter H. Tripp, insurance	69.30
Doris M. Kenison, janitor service	5.50
George P. Kelley, transportation	37.50

Maxwell A. Reid, janitor service	$5.50
Katharine Coulson, salary	85.00
Katherine Chase, salary	85.00
Loella M. Wells, salary	72.00
Olga H. Peterson, salary	65.00
Evelyn E. Clark, salary	60.00
Doris M. Kenison, salary	60.00
Robert M. Tripp, janitor service and supplies	6.57
Eleanora C. Nutter, cash paid Sadie Foss for cleaning schoolhouses	12.28
A. H. Martel, balance due on account	238.94
George P. Kelley, transportation	37.50
Reigh Carter, janitor service	14.00
Charles N. Huckins, labor	1.50
A. G. Bickford, wood for Short Falls	36.00
M. C. Philbrick, repairs at Center	30.86
Ellsworth B. Philbrick, repairs at Center	15.80
Silver Burdett & Co., text-books	12.55
American Book Co., text-books	26.28
L. H. Nutter, wood for Gossville, Center, and New Orchard	80.25
George E. Huckins, wire fence, etc.	63.54
Pembroke Water Works, water bill	7.00
Suncook Bank, 6 months interest on note	40.00
Samuel R. Yeaton, wood for New Rye	35.00
E. C. Straw, cleaning vault at New Rye	2.00
Loella M. Wells, salary	72.00
Katharine Coulson, salary	85.00
Katherine Chase, salary	85.00
Olga H. Peterson, salary	65.00
Evelyn E. Clark, salary	60.00
Doris M. Kenison, salary	60.00
George P. Kelley, transportation	45.00
Silver & Young, cement, nails, etc.	104.45
George W. Fowler, bricks for chimney	15.00

J. L. Hammett Co., supplies	$1.92
George H. Haynes, sawing three cords wood	4.50
Bickford & Huckins, fuel	22.75
Silver & Young, supplies	1.07
Loella M. Wells, salary	72.00
Katharine Coulson, salary	85.00
Katherine Chase, salary	85.00
Evelyn E. Clark, salary	60.00
Olga H. Peterson, salary	65.00
Doris M. Kenison, salary	50.00
Pittsfield School District, high school tuition, four pupils, one-half year	140.00
Geo. W. Fowler, treasurer Pembroke Academy, tuition, eight pupils, one-half year	280.00
George P. Kelley, transportation	36.25
Edson C. Eastman Co., school warrants	.37
Eldon Howard, janitor service	5.00
James E. Marden, cleaning vault at Short Falls	2.00
C. N. Huckins, labor	1.70
World Book Co., text-books	25.49
Loella M. Wells, salary	72.00
Katharine Coulson, salary	85.00
Katherine Chase, salary	85.00
Olga H. Peterson, salary	70.00
Evelyn E. Clark, salary	60.00
George P. Kelley, transportation	50.00
Raymond Hart, transportation	40.00
L. H. Nutter, seven cords wood	63.00
Lucille Marden, janitor service	3.50
Reigh Carter, janitor service	10.80
Union School District of Concord, high school tuition	105.00
Annie M. Fowler, salary as district treasurer	15.00
Eleanora C. Nutter, salary as member of school board	30.00

Grace E. Marden, salary as member of school board	$25.00
Helen T. Rand, salary as member of school board	25.00
Bickford & Huckins, shingles and lumber	116.35
American Book Co., text-books	6.64
Loella M. Wells, salary	72.00
Katharine Coulson, salary	85.00
Katherine Chase, salary	85.00
Olga H. Peterson, salary	70.00
Evelyn E. Clark, salary	60.00
George P. Kelley, transportation	50.00
Raymond Hart, transportation	40.00
Ada F. Little, cleaning New Orchard schoolhouse	5.00
Elmer H. Palmer, sawing four cords wood	6.00
William J. Rogers, sawing five cords wood	7.50
Loella M. Wells, salary	72.00
Katharine Coulson, salary	85.00
Katherine Chase, salary	85.00
Olga H. Peterson, salary	70.00
Evelyn E. Clark, salary	60.00
George P. Kelley, transportation	50.00
Raymond Hart, transportation	40.00
F. W. Saltmarsh, clerk hire for supervisory union	40.00
Eldon W. Howard, janitor service	3.50
Loella M. Wells, salary	65.00
Katharine Coulson, salary	85.00
Katherine Chase, salary	85.00
Olga H. Peterson, salary	70.00
Evelyn E. Clark, salary	60.00
George P. Kelley, transportation	25.00
Raymond Hart, transportation	20.00
Maxwell Reid, janitor service	12.50
Eldon W. Howard, janitor service	4.00
Loella M. Wells, janitor service	18.00
Loella M. Wells, balance due on salary	7.00

Eleanora C. Nutter, ribbon for diplomas	$1.62
Eleanora C. Nutter, cash paid Kenneth Osborne for janitor service	11.00
Chichester School District, tuition, three pupils	108.00
Pittsfield School District, tuition	284.00
George W. Fowler, tuition	230.00
F. W. Yeaton, taking census and services as truant officer	40.00
Total	$11,110.51

Eight pupils completed the eighth grade work last June. Graduation exercises were held at I. O. O. F. hall on June 19, 1924, with the following program:

Music	Orchestra
Invocation	Rev. George C. Junkins
Essay, Abraham Lincoln, with *Salutatory	
	Marguerite Stanley
Song	Tramp, Tramp, the Class is Marching
Essay, Our Town	Idella G. Batchelder
Piano Solo, "Pearly Dewdrops"	Bernice C. Ordway
Essay, Theodore Roosevelt	Kenneth C. Osborne
Essay, Jeffersonian Achievements	Ernest T. Taylor, Jr.
Piano Solo, "Danse d'Etoiles"	Lucille R. Marden
Essay, In the Land of Cotton	Bernice C. Ordway
Essay, In the Land of Wheat	Ethel E. Mason
Essay, In the Land of Ore	Esther R. Yeaton
Essay, New England States, with *Valedictory	
	Lucille.R. Marden
Song, Just a Song at Parting	
Address, James N. Pringle, Deputy Commissioner of Education	
Presentation of Diplomas	Supt. Henry S. Roberts
Music	Orchestra

*Salutatory and Valedictory honors were assigned by vote of the class.

During the summer various minor repairs were made. The Gossville and New Rye school buildings were painted. The interior of the New Rye schoolhouse was also painted, and needed improvements were made on the shed. The North Road schoolhouse and shed were shingled.

A wire fence was placed around the playground at Gossville in accordance with the agreement with Mr. C. S. Hall. This lot, extending northerly 200 feet with its width approximately that of the original school lot, provides an ample playground that is much appreciated. By the removal of a stone wall and by grading the bank a source of danger has been removed.

The school census, taken by Mr. F. W. Yeaton, shows that in September, 1924, there were in the district between the ages of five and sixteen years 56 boys and 53 girls, making a total of 109.

Five schools are maintained this year. The pupils living in the North Road and Center districts are assigned to Gossville. Miss Katherine Chase teaches the four lower grades again this year. Miss Olga H. Peterson was transferred from New Rye to Gossville and has charge of the higher grades. Miss Evelyn E. Clark returned to New Orchard for her second year. Two new teachers, Miss Doris E. Wadsworth and Miss Eleanor Anderson, were elected to fill vacancies at Short Falls and New Rye, respectively.

As will be seen in the table of attendance the number of cases of tardiness has decreased about one-half from the number in the report of the previous year. It is most gratifying to note this fact, and we trust that parents will continue to co-operate with the teachers in order that the best results may be obtained from our schools.

Respectfully submitted,

GRACE E. MARDEN
HELEN T. RAND
ELEANORA C. NUTTER
School Board.

REPORT OF TREASURER OF SCHOOL DISTRICT

For the Fiscal Year Ending June 30, 1924

RECEIPTS

Balance on hand, July 1, 1923	$129.59
Received from town:	
Support of schools	5,135.00
High school and academy tuition	1,000.00
Salaries, district officers	95.00
Payment of interest on debt	40.00
Payment of per capita tax	230.00
Special appropriation	800.00
Dog license money	93.04
From school board money borrowed	3,100.00
Sale of property	85.00
Lawn parties and entertainments	297.35
Towns of Allenstown and Deerfield, tuition	144.00
	$11,148.98

EXPENDITURES

Paid orders drawn by school board	$11,110.51
Balance on hand, June 30, 1924	$38.47

Respectfully submitted,

ANNIE M. FOWLER,
Treasurer.

I hereby certify that I have examined the accounts of the School Board and Treasurer of the School District for the fiscal year ending June 30, 1924, and find them correctly cast and supported by the proper vouchers.

OLIVER C. LOMBARD,

June 30, 1924.   Auditor.

I herewith submit my sixth annual report of the schools of Epsom.

There were maintained during the year, five schools for a school-year of 36 weeks and one school for 21 weeks. Short Falls school was closed on February 29 and the pupils assigned to Gossville and New Rye schools. Miss Olga Peterson, teacher at Short Falls, was transferred to the New Rye school.

The school enrollment was 111 (57 boys and 54 girls), with an average attendance of 92 per cent, making a gain of 2 per cent from last year.

The schools are in a wholesome condition, being well supplied with text-books, scholars' supplies and other equipment.

The addition of another school room at Gossville has greatly improved the school condition of the district. Two teachers are now employed, each having four grades instead of, as formerly, one teacher having eight grades.

There are 46 pupils enrolled at this school, 22 in the Primary room, 24 in the Grammar room. This arrangement gives the teachers an opportunity for a longer recitation period and also more time for assisting the individual pupils and for socialized studies.

An excellent plan was followed in making this additional room for it not only added to the usefulness of the school-plant but also to its attractiveness and beauty.

Great credit is due your school board for their labor and wisdom in the management of this work.

The liberality of Charles Sumner Hall in donating land for the enlargement of the school lot is surely appreciated by the citizens and especially by the pupils.

The School home is an important factor in the ed cation of the child and should leave a lasting impressic upon the mind for good character and citizenship.

The school building should be sanitary, comfortabl well-lighted, ventilated and heated and located on a l large enough to afford wholesome health exercises ar games.

To secure these benefits it is necessary to have tl active coöperation of the citizens, especially at the annu District Meeting when the appropriations are made.

The expenditures for the support and maintenance schools have increased, but in no greater ratio than pe sonal, business and other public expenditures.

HEALTH INSPECTION

Health inspection has been conducted yearly, defec noted and cards sent to the parents, telling them of the defects and urging remedial treatment. A few paren have heeded this advice and had these defects correcte benefitting the child both as to health and to learnii ability. The greater number of parents apparently p no attention to these cards, as the pupils return wi adenoids, decayed teeth and enlarged tonsils.

If the danger of these defects to the child's physic and mental welfare is understood by the parents, would seem that they would seek proper medical tre ment.

Adenoids and bad tonsils are sources of dangerc diseases and are directly responsible for the backwa ness of many pupils.

Many children have defective vision, which the medi inspector notes on the cards. Parents should be anxic to provide properly fitted glasses for such, as eye-str causes headaches and affects the nervous system a general health of the child.

Of 432,000 school children who were examined in one of the New England states more than one in five had defective vision.

TEACHERS' MEETINGS

The teachers' meetings held during the year have been well attended.

At one meeting Commissioner E. W. Butterfield gave his interesting lecture on the Law of Heredity. At another Supt. Morris, of Manchester, and Assistant Supt. Walker, of Concord, talked on the Standardized Tests. Both speakers interested and instructed the teachers. Their talks were especially helpful at that time as the teachers were about to use the Courtis Standard Practice Tests in Arithmetic.

I have found the teachers industrious and working for the best interest of the pupils.

REPORT CARDS

I would urge the parents to examine carefully the report cards brought home by their children and to confer with the teacher upon any item on the card not understood. These cards are a record of the child's attendance, conduct, effort and scholarship.

Parents and citizens are cordially invited to visit the schools frequently that they may get an accurate knowledge of the work of the school-room.

In conclusion I express my appreciation for your cooperation and assistance.

Respectfully submitted,

HENRY S. ROBERTS.

ROLL OF PERFECT ATTENDANCE

Pupils neither absent nor tardy during the year ending June 30, 1924:

NEW ORCHARD

Orville S. Bickford   John B. Yeaton

SCHOOL CALENDAR, 1925-1926

September 8, 1925, to December 18, 1925   14 weeks
Thanksgiving Recess, November 20 to November 30
January 4, 1926, to February 19, 1926   7 weeks
March 1, 1926, to April 16, 1926   7 weeks
April 26, 1926, to June 18, 1926   8 weeks

NO-SCHOOL DAYS

September 7   Fast Day
October 12   Memorial Day
                                     Institute Days

NAMES OF HIGH SCHOOL STUDENTS

CONCORD HIGH SCHOOL

Arthur G. Huckins   Claude H. Huckins

Kenneth M. Hnckins

PITTSFIELD HIGH SCHOOL

Hattie E. Ambrose   Allan P. Barton

Clara M. Bickford   Kenneth A. Reid

PEMBROKE ACADEMY

George O. Moulton   Helen M. Skinner

Gladys M. Moulton   Howard W. Tallman

Ray F. Murby   Leroy A. Taylor

Dean E. Ordway   Richard G. Worth

ATTENDANCE TABLE FOR THE SCHOOL YEAR ENDING JUNE 30, 1924

Number of schools	No. half days school was in session	No. half days lost	Number of tardinesses	No. of half days attendance	No. of half days absence	Visits by Superintendent	Visits by School Board	Visits by citizens	Pupils not absent or tardy	No. Pupils Registered, not Registered Elsewhere — Boys	Girls	Total	Whole No. of Pupils Registered — Boys	Girls	Total	Non-residence	Average daily attendance	Average daily absence	Average membership	Per cent. of attendance	Attendance in another Public School in District — Boys	Girls	Total
1	203	7	12	1,194	136	5	4	52	0	5	8	13	5	8	13	0	5.88	.66	6.54	90	0	0	0
1	350	10	23	6,479	345	11	5	23	0	11	8	19	13	10	23	1	18.51	.98	19.49	95	2	1	3
1	348	12	33	5,539	681	13	5	49	0	10	7	17	12	11	23	0	15.91	1.95	17.86	89	2	3	5
1	348	12	20	6,489	657	13	5	27	0	9	10	19	11	14	25	0	18.65	1.89	20.54	90	2	4	6
1	348	12	12	3,362	114	10	2	16	2	7	3	10	7	3	10	0	9.66	.34	10.00	96	0	0	0
1	350	10	38	5,232	514	10	5	66	0	9	7	16	9	8	17	3	14.96	1.47	16.43	91	0	0	0
6	1,947	63	138	28,295	2,447	62	26	233	2	51	43	94	57	54	111	4	87.19	7.54	94.73	92	6	8	14

REPORT OF THE PUBLIC LIBRARY TRUSTEES

The Trustees of the Epsom Public Library herewith present this report of the financial condition of, and expenditures for, the library during the year ending January 31st, 1925, and the librarian's report and record for the same period.

We do not list the books added during the year, acting under the impression that its cost is not justified in view of the installation of the new card indexing system. The indexing of the books of the library is progressing favorably in charge of Miss Doris E. Burnham, the librarian, assisted by Miss Hester Bickford.

The library has been painted during the year, and an appropriate sign has been affixed to the building.

We gratefully acknowledge the gift of two books of fiction from Mrs. Harold C. Brown of this town; and, from the Carnegie Endowment for International Peace, the gifts of sixteen volumes for our International Mind Alcove, and other booklets and pamphlets; and, from Henry Ford, of Detroit, Michigan, his usual yearly subscription to the "Dearborn Independent."

Respectfully submitted,

JOHN W. GRIFFIN,
WARREN TRIPP,
HELEN M. LOMBARD,

Trustees.

January 31, 1925.

FINANCIAL STATEMENT

RECEIPTS

Balance from last year	$46.93
Trustees of trust funds	150.00
Town of Epsom, for painting	150.00
Town of Epsom, for card indexing system	100.00
Town of Epsom, for maintenance	60.00
Cash from fines	12.49
Librarian's cash on hand, January, 1924	7.05
	$526.47

PAYMENTS

Painting and varnishing library (by contract)	$100.00
Sign on library building	10.00
Repairs on porch and building	9.30
Library Bureau, card indexing apparatus	80.50
Shoveling snow	1.20
Granite Monthly, subscription	2.00
Educators' Association, "The Volume Library"	11.00
A. N. Marquis, "Who's Who in America," Vol. 13	6.98
W. P. Goodman, books	52.22
Doris E. Burnham, services to Jan. 1, 1925	40.00
Portieres, fixtures and poles	13.55
Library incidentals	4.45
Cash in hands of librarian	1.54
Balance on hand	193.13
	$526.47

Amount in hands of Trustees of Trust Funds available for book purchases	$436.57

LIBRARY ENDOWMENT FUNDS

Dr. Orrin S. Sanders fund	$100.00
Mary A. Evans fund	500.00
Benjamin F. Webster fund	1,000.00
Susan E. P. Forbes fund	2,000.00
Total	$3,600.00

LIBRARIAN'S RECORD

Number of books owned by library, about	2,869
Active borrowers	250
Number of volumes non-fiction lent	637
Number of volumes fiction lent	1,637
Number of unbound periodicals lent	15
Total circulation	2,289
Number of books added, exclusive of public documents	89

PUBLIC LIBRARY TRUSTEES

John W. Griffin   Warren Tripp

Helen M. Lombard

LIBRARIAN

Doris E. Burnham

Residence	Name of child	Sex	All Living	No.	Name of father	Name of mother	All White	Residence of parents	Occupation of father	Birthplace of father	Birthplace of mother
psom	Gordon N.	M		3	Charles N. Huckins	Doris E. Waterhouse		Epsom	Ato Dealer	Deerfield	Epsom
"	Leonard Allen	M		5	Eugene H. ...Mick	Lizzie E. Pickard		"	Farmer	California	Deerfield
"	Lois Evelyn	F		2	William ...ib.	Amy O. Kimball		"	Weaver	Suncook	Lakeport
"	Carroll Dustin	M		1	Chester Y. Batchelder ...Gus	Alice V. Dow		"	Farmer	Epsom	Northwood
"	Harvey W. ...Nalie	M		1	Lois A. Demers	Harriett L. Harvey		"	Clerk	...	...
"	Kathleen ...Nalie	F		2	Arthur ...arne	...e S Small		"	Farmer	...	Pittsfield
"	Grace Eleanor	F		7	John P. Yeaton	Hazel V. Bailey		"	Laborer	Northwood	Temple
"	Cath'rine Frances	F		1	Walter E. Pickard	...sie M. McKenzie		"	Farmer	Canterbury	Tilton
"	Walter H.	M		3	Olin L. ...avis	Ida M. Shaw		"	Laborer	Epsom	Deerfield
"	R ger ...holm	M		5	Elbridge M. Bartlett	Ruth D. Kimball		"	Poultryman	Manchester	Epsom
"	Carroll Frederick	M		1	George H. Quimby	Mable N. ...B.		"	Farmer	Springfield	"
"	Lillian Ellis	F		5	Fred C. Fife	Lena Stone		"	Laborer	Epsom	Roxbury, Mass.
oncord	Nancy	F		3	Oliver C. Lombard	Ernestine ...iny		"	Poultryman	Roxbury, Mass.	Roxbury, Mass.
psom	Marie Arline	F		1	Edgar A. Stevens	Ruth A. Pike		"	Merchant	Contoocook	Epsom
						Helen J. Morey			Laborer		

I hereby certify that the above return is correct, according to the best of my knowledge and belief.

MAURICE C. PHILBRICK, *Town Clerk.*

Place of marriage	Name	Residence	Age	Color	Occupation	Birthplace	Names of parents	Birthplace of parents	Occupation of parents	No.	Officiating clergyman and residence
Chichester	Percy K. Elliott	Epsom	24	All White	Farmer	Hooksett	Charles E. Elliott	Deerfield	Farmer	1	Rev. John H. Vinc... Chichester
							Phœbe J. Bickford	Epsom	Home		
	Loella M. Perkins	"	17		Domestic	Northwood	Joseph Perkins	Barrington	Laborer	1	
							Lizzie Richardson	Northwood	Home		
Pittsfield	Edgar Aaron Stevens	Chichester	18		Teamster	Contoocook	Edgar Stevens	Boston, Mass.	Clerk	1	Rev. C. Wendall Wils... Pittsfield
							Margaret McDonald	Prince Edw. Is.	Home		
	Ruth A. Pike	Epsom	17		Waitress	Epsom	George V. Pike	H'wk'nsvill, Ga	Farmer	1	
						[Mass.]	Ethel Marden	Epsom	Home		
Pittsfield	Percival R. Eaton	"	64		Farmer	So. Reading	Edwin A. Eaton	Boston, Mass.	Clergyman	2	Rev. W. I. Sweet Pittsfield
						[Mich.]	Sarah Slocomb	Haverhill, Mass	Artist		
	Lillian Adams Reid	"	50		Home	Battle Creek	Onyx Adams	Check'rbury, Vt	Farmer	2	
							Bessie Wickware	Colchester, Vt.	Home		
Manchester	Edwin L. Bunker	"	37		Farmer	Pittsfield	James V. Bunker	Barnstead	Farmer	2	Rev. J. Wesley Raf... Manchester
							Sarah M. Swain	Chichester	Home		
	Loella M. Wells	"	49		Teacher	Epsom	Freeman Marden	Epsom	Millman	2	
							Lovina I. Bickford	Lowell, Mass.	Home		
Suncook	Paul Kamper	"	28		Weaver	Germany	Adolph Kamper	Germany	Weaver	1	Rev. C. P. Buck Catholic Priest Suncook
							Marie Miller	Manchester	Home.. [man		
	Gertrude Lillian Ryalls	Manchester	19		Waitress	Manchester	James E. Ryalls	Manchester	R. R. Switch-	1	
							Annie G. Mills	England	Home		
Chichester	Walter A. Sawyer	Epsom	31		Mechanic	Concord	James W. Sawyer	Dunbarton	Cook	1	Rev. Addison F. Giff... Chichester
							Ellen L. Webber	Concord	Home		
	Eliza Wheeler	"	19		Home	Epsom	Frank P. Wheeler	Norwich, Vt.	Farmer	1	
							Lillian C. Hilliard	Chichester	Home		

I hereby certify that the above return is correct, according to the best of my knowledge and belief.

M. C. PHILBRICK, *Town Clerk.*

Place of death	Name and surname of deceased	Age. Years	Age. Months	Age. Days	Place of birth	Sex	Color	Sin., mar. or wid'd.	Occupation.	Place of birth. Father.	Place of birth. Mother.	Name of father.	Maiden name of mother.
Epsom	True W. Center	84	3	22	Loudon	M	White	W	None	Suncook	Deerfield	Abel M. Center	Lois ——
"	Lois Evelyn Duhaime			5	Epsom [C'n	F	White	S	"	Canada	Canada	William Duhaime	Amy O. Kimball
"	Arthur Stone	43	9		St. Agate,	M	White	M	Poultrym'n	Meredith	Belmont	Joseph Desrosier	Sophronia
"	Albert E. Dow	57			Laconia,	M	White	D	Carpenter	Epsom	Chichester	Lawrence Dow	Mary Libby
"	Lizzie G. Bickford	74	8	20	Epsom	F	White	M	Home	Deerfield		William Goss	Maryetta Abbott
"	Rufus B. Doe	87	4	2	Deerfield	M	White	W	None	Northwood	Northwood	Joseph A. Doe	Mary E. Drew
"	Ida E. Lakin	69	6	23	Northwood	F	White	W	"			Charles Winslow	Hannah Watson
"	Ellen L. Sawyer	71	2	19	Concord	F	White	D	Home	Bow	Concord	John B. Webber	Rhoda Simpson
"	Sherman W. Lewis	67			Barnstead	M	White	S	Care Taker	Ellsworth		Daniel N. Lewis	

I hereby certify that the above return is correct, according to the best of my knowledge and belief.

M. D. PHILBRICK, *Town Clerk.*

Bodies Brought to Epsom for Interment for the Year ending December 31, 1924.

Date of death	Place of death	Name and surname of the deceased	Sex	Age			Name of father	Maiden name of mother.
				Years.	Months.	Days.		
1924								
Feb. 21	Indian Head, Md.	Clayton H. Fowler	M	44	1	15	Horace Fowler	Ida Holt
Mar. 5	Pembroke	Kate E. Dolbeer	F	81	11	15	Benj. M. Towle	Hannah Sanborn
Apr. 28	Boston, Mass.	George D. Yeaton	M	63	8	9	Benj. B. Yeaton	Mary F. James
May 19	Fitchburg, Mass.	Anna T. Knox	F	68	11	2		
July 26	Gonic	Myra C. Billings	F	55	8	20	Freeman Tuttle	Jane Cassell
Oct. 3	Hazelton, Pa.	Harold Brown	M	36			Frank Brown	Nellie Dow
10	Westford, Mass.	Sarah Jane Marsh	F			1		
16	Concord	Eleanor Yeaton	F		9	5		
22	Pittsfield	Josephine A. Warren	F	20			Joseph A. Warren	Lucy A. Heacock
	Saugus, Mass.	Josiah Smith	M					

I hereby certify that the above return is correct, according to the best of my knowledge and belief.

M. C. PHILBRICK, *Town Clerk.*

Lightning Source UK Ltd.
Milton Keynes UK
UKHW020808221118
332756UK00019B/1971/P